THE DEVIL'S WIFE (LA ESPOSA DEL DIABLO)

Tom Jacobson

BROADWAY PLAY PUBLISHING INC
New York
www.broadwayplaypublishing.com
info@broadwayplaypublishing.com

Cover photo by Ed Krieger

First edition: October 2017
I S B N: 978-0-88145-734-6

Book design: Marie Donovan
Page make-up: Adobe InDesign
Typeface: Palatino

THE DEVIL'S WIFE opened on 15 July 2017 at
Skylight Theatre in Los Angeles, produced by Gary
Grossman and Tony Abatemarco. The cast and creative
contributors were:

BONITA .... Mariel Neto
DULCE..Alana Dietze
SOFIA..Carolyn Zeller
NICOLAS/RATEL.. Everette Wallin

Director..Eric Hoff
Set design..................................Stephanie Kerley-Schwartz
Lighting design .... Jeff McLaughlin
Sound design................................Christopher Moscatiello
Costume design..................................Sarah Figoten Wilson
Production stage manager .... Christopher Hoffman
Publicity... Judith Borne
Associate producer .... Jonathan Muñoz-Proulx

CHARACTERS & SETTING

Bonita Ramirez, *the oldest daughter, beautiful*
Dulce Ramirez, *the middle daughter, pretty*
Sofia Ramirez, *the youngest daughter*
Nicolas Mastema, *an attorney, also plays:* Ratel, *an elderly servant*

The action takes place on the Ramirez *and* Mastema *estates.*

And hell.

The time is whenever. Possibly Medieval Europe, Mexico or Los Angeles in the mid-nineteenth century, or today.

The two estate interiors can be realistic or stylized, perhaps hardly different except for one or two details of decor. As for hell, go crazy.

(*Thunder.* SOFIA RAMIREZ, *an attractive young woman dressed in wet but formal mourning, practices self-defense moves with a large wooden staff. She's impressive. Her sisters* BONITA *and* DULCE *enter, also dressed in mourning, also rather wet. They watch her a moment.*)

BONITA: (*Shaking head*) So embarrassing.

SOFIA: (*Keeps practicing*) Orphans have to protect themselves.

DULCE: Sofia, he's been in the ground less than half an hour.

BONITA: Completely disrespectful.

SOFIA: Much can be accomplished with a good, stout stick, as father always said.

BONITA: He never said that.

DULCE: It sounds like something he'd say, though.

SOFIA: I'm preparing for our future. It's not as if he left us well-provided for.

BONITA: That's an understatement!

DULCE: The flood was not his fault.

BONITA: Nor the drought. Nor the locusts.

SOFIA: Nor the lawyers.

DULCE: We still have the estate!

BONITA: And all its expenses.

SOFIA: And taxes. On thirty-five thousand acres.

BONITA: Thirty-three.

DULCE: What?

BONITA: Papa sold the parcel across the river six weeks ago.

DULCE: And never told us?

BONITA: He knew you'd be upset, so he asked me not to tell you. At least he got a little gold for it.

SOFIA: That'll last us what, six months?

BONITA: Not even. He had to discount the land—subject to flooding. Especially today.

DULCE: That's all you care about—

DULCE: Money!   SOFIA: Gold!

BONITA: I care about security! For all of us! *(Grabbing the staff)* Give me that! Where'd you get that dirty thing?

SOFIA: Father gave it to me! Let go!

(Knocks her deftly away)

DULCE: He gave it to you?

SOFIA: As he lay dying.

BONITA: Why? What did he say?

SOFIA: Nothing—he was in   DULCE: How awful you
too much pain—   were the only one with
                                him—!

BONITA: So sudden—his   SOFIA: He just handed it
heart—!   to me—and the look in
                                his eyes—! *(Weeps)*

BONITA: There, there, dear.

DULCE: Let her cry! We're in mourning, for God's sake!

BONITA: Yes, cry it out, just don't let the servants see you.

SOFIA: We don't have any servants.

DULCE: I'm sure we will again soon!

BONITA: We'll have to sell a few more parcels.

(Gestures to DULCE, *who helps her undress)*

DULCE: But this is our home! Our legacy! Surely there are other ways. We're three pretty girls—we have lots of assets of our own!

BONITA: I will not be pandered!

DULCE: *(Undressing with* BONITA'*s help)* Of course not, dear! We wouldn't want you to blow the dust off your famous virtue. I, on the other hand, am perfectly willing to sacrifice myself for the family.

BONITA: You're always willing, aren't you, dear?

SOFIA: Father said the oldest must marry first.

DULCE: Father's gone. And I can't sit around waiting till Bonita thaws herself out.

BONITA: I'm sorry, but Sofia's right. It's only proper I marry first, as much as I loathe the idea. I'm willing to put up with a husband if it means security for all of us. But what could I bring as dowry?

SOFIA: She is the most beautiful.

DULCE: Ah, yes, very true.

BONITA: I'm no prettier than you—I just take care of myself.

DULCE: But as the oldest, your charms will be the first to fade.

BONITA: Your asset is your sweet temperament.

SOFIA: Ah, yes, very true.

DULCE & BONITA: *(Very quickly)* And you're the most—

BONITA: Intelligent!   DULCE: Clever!

SOFIA: Not that intelligence and cleverness hold any value in this shallow world.

DULCE: I'm sure there's a man out there who would appreciate you.

BONITA: At least one.

SOFIA: We can't just sit here waiting for Bonita to marry or worthless land to sell.

BONITA: Figure something out then, smartie.

SOFIA: I have.

DULCE: Oh, dear.   BONITA: Oh, no.

SOFIA: We're beautiful, sweet and clever, but we have no sophistication when it comes to real estate law. We need an attorney.

BONITA: Not another horrid old lawyer!

SOFIA: He'll be here shortly.

BONITA: Sofia, we need to make these kinds of decisions together now that Papa's gone, not ad hoc.

DULCE: Is he handsome?

BONITA: Oh, Dulce!

SOFIA: I haven't met him. He contacted me when he heard Father died.

BONITA: Parasite! No doubt he's seventy-nine with scrofula.

SOFIA: And three teeth!

BONITA: Gout!

DULCE: Girls in our situation need to keep their options open.

BONITA: Dear, your options are always open.

DULCE: Mean!

SOFIA: We mustn't fight. Our best asset is each other.

DULCE & BONITA: Ah, yes, very true.

(Thunder. They jump.)

DULCE: Goodness! Peculiar weather. Such brilliant sun!

(SOFIA *throws open a window. Sunlight streams into the room. Sound of rain and more thunder.*)

BONITA: Such heavy rain!

SOFIA: The Devil is beating his wife.

BONITA: What?

SOFIA: It's an old saying.

DULCE: That doesn't make any sense. Why would a sunshower mean the Devil is beating his wife? Who believes in the Devil any more, anyway?

BONITA: I do. The world is inherently evil.

DULCE: No! More good than evil. You only see the rain, Bonita! Look at that beautiful sun, birds, bunnies—

SOFIA: You only see the sun, Dulce!

BONITA: And the heaviest rain can't wash the world clean of cruelty, humiliation and pain.

DULCE: I want to experience every sensation life has to offer. Even pain!

BONITA: Pain comes from the Devil.

DULCE: I'd sooner believe in God than the Devil!

BONITA: How can you believe in God after all that's happened? Floods, droughts—

SOFIA: Locusts—

BONITA & SOFIA: Lawyers—

BONITA: Papa's death?

DULCE: But the drought's over! It's raining right now!

(*Rain stops*)

DULCE: Well, it was. (*Looks out the window*) I wonder if there's a rainbow. (*Closes window*)

SOFIA: The world is neither bad nor good. It just is. Don't you remember what Father said?

BONITA: I miss him terribly!

DULCE: Don't! I'm just barely holding myself together.

SOFIA: "There is no God: natural beings support themselves."

DULCE: If he said that it was only to shock people.

BONITA: I'm sure he believed in the Devil.

SOFIA: I believe in neither God nor the Devil.

DULCE: What do you believe in?

SOFIA: Truth.

DULCE: Truth without meaning? Without God?

SOFIA: You want meaning? In this world?

BONITA: Dulce, you always ask for too much.

DULCE: There has to be God! There has to be meaning! Otherwise, what are we here for?

SOFIA: That's called theodicy.

DULCE: Oh, I hate that poem. So many ridiculous monsters.

SOFIA: Not *The Odyssey*! Theodicy!

BONITA: Spell it.

SOFIA: T-H-E-O-D-I-C-Y. The search for justice in the universe.

BONITA: Oh. It's idiocy, but with God in it.

DULCE: You're both impossible! We're sisters—

BONITA & SOFIA: Half!   DULCE: —But nothing
                                      alike!

DULCE: Optimism is my nature. My mother ate lots of honey when she was pregnant with me, which is why I'm sweet. Bonita's mother filled the house with flowers before you were born, so you turned out beautiful and pure.

SOFIA: And my mother?

DULCE: She…read a lot of books.

(By now DULCE *and* BONITA *are both undressed down to their underwear, but* SOFIA *is still clothed. There is a knock at the door.)*

SOFIA: That's the attorney! Go put some clothes on!

DULCE: *(Re: the discarded clothes)* Why haven't the servants—?

BONITA & SOFIA: We don't have any servants!

*(*BONITA *and* DULCE *quickly gather their discarded clothing and disappear.* SOFIA *rests the staff against the wall and answers the door.)*

SOFIA: Welcome, sir.

*(*NICOLAS MASTEMA *comes into the house. He's well dressed, slightly imperious.)*

NICOLAS: Are the Ramirez sisters home? They are expecting me— *(He gives her a card)* Nicolas Mastema, esquire.

SOFIA: Very nice to meet you, Mr Mastema. I'm Sofia Ramirez.

NICOLAS: Answering your own door? Haven't you servants?

SOFIA: Precisely why we are in need of your services. We have thirty-five—no, thirty-three—thousand acres but can't afford to staff a household.

NICOLAS: My apologies—and my condolences. You are in mourning.

SOFIA: Yes, we buried Father an hour ago.

NICOLAS: A remarkable man. Famous for his radical thinking.

SOFIA: We are proud to be his daughters.

NICOLAS: I debated him once. A formidable opponent.

SOFIA: He never lost an argument.

NICOLAS: You must miss him very much, the blow so fresh. *(He produces a flower, almost as if by magic, but casually, not with showmanship.)*

SOFIA: Oh, gorgeous!

NICOLAS: My modest memorial to your renowned parent.

SOFIA: How very thoughtful, especially for a meeting that's professional, not personal, in nature.

NICOLAS: My firm specializes in the personal touch.

SOFIA: May I get you something? Coffee? Tea?

NICOLAS: I'd enjoy a glass of wine, but only if you'll join me.

SOFIA: Wine, at a business meeting?

NICOLAS: It's your personal business we're discussing.

SOFIA: *(Pours two glasses)* I admire your approach to business, sir.

(NICOLAS and SOFIA drink and look at each other.)

NICOLAS: You're wet.

SOFIA: That sudden downpour.

(NICOLAS and SOFIA drink and look at each other.)

NICOLAS: Your father recently sold two-thousand acres across the river?

SOFIA: Yes.

NICOLAS: He could have gotten a better price, I hear. River access.

SOFIA: But dry since the drought. You can't water with dust.

NICOLAS: Wells can be drilled.

SOFIA: We had a well there. It didn't help.

NICOLAS: Probably too shallow. You can drill much deeper.

SOFIA: But after regular expenses, we have little capital left for drilling.

NICOLAS: And with the rain today, perhaps your river will flow again.

(NICOLAS *and* SOFIA *look at each other, sipping.*)

SOFIA: And in any case, that land is sold. Water under the bridge.

NICOLAS: Drilling may save your remaining acres. (*Pulls out papers*) I have a proposal—

SOFIA: We should wait for my sisters. They'll be down shortly.

NICOLAS: Of course. The Ramirez sisters are nearly as famous as their father—

SOFIA: Oh, hardly!

NICOLAS: Bonita is a great beauty.

SOFIA: She is. Wait till you see her.

NICOLAS: And known for her acts of charity, goodness and virtue.

SOFIA: She's sort of perfect. It's annoying.

NICOLAS: And Dulce? Is she truly as sweet-tempered, kind and thoughtful as they say?

SOFIA: You make her sound simple-minded.

NICOLAS: Kindness is the greatest wisdom.

(NICOLAS *and* SOFIA *sip.*)

SOFIA: And Sofia?

NICOLAS: The youngest sister?

SOFIA: Yes. What do they say of her?

NICOLAS: She's a bit more complicated.

SOFIA: Is she sweet? Is she beautiful?

NICOLAS: Well—

SOFIA: Don't hedge.

NICOLAS: She's adept in several languages.

SOFIA: *Mais oui.*

NICOLAS: And an intellectual powerhouse! Her commentary on Cervantes is the envy of many a scholar.

SOFIA: You've read her work?

NICOLAS: I read everything. She impressed me, which isn't easy.

SOFIA: She must be hideous.

NICOLAS: No, no—physically, she's—

(SOFIA *jumps up and grabs her staff.*)

SOFIA: Athletic? Skillful? (*Makes some moves, threatening him playfully with the staff*) Aggressive?

NICOLAS: She's best known for her sense of humor. Tart.

SOFIA: Her mother drank a lot of vinegar during pregnancy.

NICOLAS: Where'd you get that staff?

SOFIA: It was Father's.

NICOLAS: It's actually mine. He won it from me in a bet.

SOFIA: It was important to him. It has special powers.

NICOLAS: Special powers? Really?

SOFIA: Wards off men.

NICOLAS: It's a perfectly ordinary wooden staff, but it's been in my family since the dawn of time. Lots of history. May I have it back? *(Reaches for it)*

SOFIA: *(Pulling it away)* Perhaps as payment for good lawyering.

NICOLAS: It has great sentimental value, but no measurable worth.

SOFIA: We'll see.

(BONITA *and* DULCE *arrive, both looking lovely.*)

SOFIA: Nicolas Mastema esquire, may I introduce my sisters Bonita—

NICOLAS: Beautiful!

SOFIA: And Dulce.

NICOLAS: So sweet.

BONITA: Lovely to meet you, Mr Mastema.

NICOLAS: Please call me Nicolas.

DULCE: Why he has hardly any scrofula at all!

NICOLAS: Scrofula?

SOFIA: My sisters are also tart.

BONITA: Dulce especially.

SOFIA: Behave, both of you. Nicolas has a proposal for us—

DULCE: A proposal? We've just met!

SOFIA: His firm has a proposal regarding our financial dilemma.

BONITA: Mr Mastema, I'm obliged to tell you my sister acted precipitously inviting you here. We have no money for your fee.

NICOLAS: I'm sure we can work something out.

DULCE: Of course, we can.

SOFIA: All we have is land.

DULCE: That's not the way!

SOFIA: Dulce's sentimental about the estate, our thirty-five thousand acre headache.

DULCE: Thirty-three thousand acre—!

NICOLAS: My proposal involves the land, of course. But you have other things of value.

DULCE: Our family name, for instance? We have deep roots, very prominent. That means a lot around here, a good alliance.

BONITA: *(To* SOFIA*)* Hit her with that stick.

NICOLAS: Why, you've just outlined the entire proposal!

BONITA, DULCE, SOFIA: What?

NICOLAS: It's three parts.

BONITA: How much land?

NICOLAS: Eleven thousand acres.

BONITA: That's a third of what remains!

NICOLAS: Hear me out.

DULCE: What else?

NICOLAS: I know this will seem very abrupt, but you are in an emergency situation, and traditionally legal marriage is based on the transfer of property—

BONITA: Marriage?!

DULCE: Sold!

BONITA: The stick!

SOFIA: As a matter of fact, Nicolas, we were discussing marriage as a solution to our dilemma just before you arrived.

NICOLAS: Please, call me Nick. Since we're to be married.

DULCE: Who will be married?

SOFIA: Which?

BONITA: What? There's no dowry, so you can stop right there.

NICOLAS: With this marriage, the eleven thousand acres functions as a dowry but stays in the family as community property. You lose nothing, and gain an in-law and financial security.

BONITA: Financial security?

DULCE: Pardon me, but whose marriage?

BONITA: Dulce, please—!

DULCE: Oh, hush, Bonita! We don't have time to be all proper—it is a fiscal emergency as Nick has so forcefully and charmingly stated. Who is the bride and who is the groom?

NICOLAS: I'm the groom, of course.

BONITA, DULCE, SOFIA: *(After a moment)* And?

NICOLAS: The bride?

DULCE: Yes?!

NICOLAS: Isn't that obvious? Of course, it's—

SOFIA: Bonita.

(They all stare at her)

SOFIA: She's the eldest. It was our father's dying wish that the eldest marry first. And the three of us agreed to that less than fifteen minutes ago.

(They all stare at SOFIA.)

SOFIA: Didn't we, girls?

BONITA: Yes—

DULCE: We did, but—

SOFIA: As this is a legal matter, we are obligated to honor the wishes of our beloved parent.

DULCE: Ah, yes, that's true.

BONITA: *(After a moment)* I hope I will be acceptable barter in this transaction, Mr Mastema.

NICOLAS: Please, Nick.

BONITA: We accept your proposal. If the collateral is worthy.

NICOLAS: Most worthy, Miss Ramirez.

BONITA: Please, Bonita.

NICOLAS: Miss Bonita. And that's assuming someone of your background is not compromised by marrying an attorney.

BONITA: Not compromised at all, Mr Nick.

NICOLAS: I'm delighted. Here's the paperwork.

SOFIA: You had it all drawn up in advance, how lawyerly.

DULCE: And confident.

NICOLAS: You need only fill in your names and sign.

SOFIA: All of us?

NICOLAS: The eleven thousand acres are your joint property.

(They all sign.)

NICOLAS: Oh, and the third stipulation!

SOFIA: Is it already written in?

NICOLAS: No, but I'll add it if you consent.

SOFIA: What is it?

NICOLAS: That staff, your stick. It's an heirloom of my family, and I'd appreciate its return.

SOFIA: Of course. No need to write it in. *(Hands him the staff)* A wedding gift.

BONITA: *(Signs)* You can come visit it, if you've become attached.

(Thunder and sudden lighting change isolates the three sisters in light as NICOLAS disappears in the darkness. DULCE and SOFIA adjust BONITA's clothing, turning her into a bride.)

DULCE: Are you sure you're all right?

BONITA: It's my responsibility. The land stays in the family, and Nicolas will support us all. His practice is quite successful, I understand. *(She bursts into tears)*

DULCE: Oh, sweetie, you know I would have—!

SOFIA: Both of us—!

DULCE: Remember, Bonita: every man comes with a convenient little handle. Get a good grip on that and they're easy to control.

BONITA: *(Shaking head)* So vulgar.

SOFIA: I'm sure he'll be the perfect husband.

DULCE: He couldn't be more handsome!

SOFIA: And kind! He solved our problem for us!

DULCE: *(Stepping away from BONITA)* Our worries are over!

SOFIA: *(Stepping away from BONITA)* That's right, no worries!

BONITA: No worries ever again.

(Thunder and lighting change. Her sisters are gone, and BONITA stands in her wedding attire in the home of

NICOLAS. *Before her stands* NICOLAS' *bent, elderly and bearded servant,* RATEL.)

RATEL: The master will be here shortly, mistress. Is there anything you need?

BONITA: No, I'm fine. Just send a maid to help me undress.

RATEL: That would be me.

BONITA: You're the maid?

RATEL: The master's needs are simple. I'm his only servant.

BONITA: Never mind. *(Removes some parts of her wedding dress)* I've grown accustomed to undressing myself.

RATEL: Perhaps the master can help you. It is your wedding night.

BONITA: What's your name again?

RATEL: Ratel, mistress.

BONITA: Ratel, please let Mr Mastema know I need to have a bath—

RATEL: Certainly! I'll draw it right—

BONITA: No! I can draw my own bath. And no need for "master" and "mistress". It's old fashioned and creepy.

RATEL: The master likes things old fashioned and creepy. And by the way, he says you may do as you wish here, as long as you abide by one rule.

BONITA: What is that?

RATEL: You must never go in the cellar. *(Points to a door)*

BONITA: Why not?

RATEL: Because he says so.

BONITA: That's hardly a reason.

RATEL: It's arbitrary and controlling, but that's how he is.

BONITA: You're a singularly disrespectful servant. How does Mr Mastema tolerate such boldness?

RATEL: I know a lot about him.

BONITA: Please let him know I'm exhausted by the wedding, the travel, and general anxiety. I beg his indulgence and wish to postpone our wedding night until I'm more rested.

RATEL: Ah. I had heard the mistress was renowned for her virtue.

BONITA: Insolence!

RATEL: I know a lot about you, too.

(Lighting change, and BONITA *is back home with* DULCE *and* SOFIA.*)*

SOFIA: Well?

BONITA: The house is very nice, a lot like ours in fact, but very isolated, and there's only one servant, a frightful hunched-up gnome with a dreadful tongue on him.

DULCE: Speaking of tongues?

BONITA: *(Shaking head)* So disgusting! Nothing's happened yet.

DULCE: Nothing?! He's such a looker! And very well put together!

BONITA: I'm not ready.

DULCE: You're afraid you'll get pregnant aren't you? Which would ruin your looks!

BONITA: He's been very understanding.

SOFIA: But you're going to have to...you know... sometime.

DULCE: I could go to your house dressed as you.

BONITA: That's very generous of you, dear, but I think he'd figure it out.

SOFIA: Is he as smart as he seems? We had a lively conversation when we first met.

BONITA: He's hardly around. Just me and that servant. And the forbidden cellar.

SOFIA: What's that?

DULCE: A forbidden cellar!? What's down there?

SOFIA: His wife before you? Or what's left of her?

DULCE: More likely his ill-gotten gains from illicit lawsuits!

BONITA: Probably nothing. Just some kind of test of my loyalty. I don't care what's in it, really.

DULCE: Probably enough to gold pay all our taxes and bring back our servants.

BONITA: I'm not stealing from my own husband!

DULCE: No, of course, not.

SOFIA: I wonder if my stick's down there.

DULCE: It's half yours anyway, community property.

(Lighting change, and BONITA *is back with* RATEL *in the* MASTEMA *house.)*

RATEL: The master requests your presence in his bed tonight.

BONITA: Could he not ask me himself?

RATEL: He's embarrassed.

BONITA: It's more embarrassing that he makes you ask. Do you know why he doesn't want me to open that door?

RATEL: Yes.

BONITA: Why?

RATEL: The consequences would be unfortunate.

BONITA: For me? For him?

RATEL: For everyone. But mostly you. Unless he doesn't find out.

BONITA: How would he know?

(RATEL *shrugs*)

BONITA: Would you tell him?

RATEL: No.

BONITA: Are you telling the truth?

RATEL: I wouldn't tell him if you opened the door.

BONITA: When is he next away?

RATEL: He has business in the city a week from Wednesday.

BONITA: My sisters are much more curious than I.

RATEL: He says you may do as you wish once you've become a proper wife.

BONITA: What does that mean? I'm quite proper!

RATEL: If it's your time of the month, the master won't mind.

BONITA: You're a vile little creature, aren't you?

RATEL: He likes blood.

(*Lighting change, and* BONITA *is back with her sisters in the* RAMIREZ *house.*)

BONITA: I told him it was my time.

DULCE: For six weeks?

SOFIA: Does he understand biology?

BONITA: He's very understanding and patient.

DULCE: I'm not! What's behind that door?

BONITA: I won't go sneaking behind my husband's back to satisfy your curiosity, you cat!

SOFIA: Dulce, you're just jealous!

DULCE: At least she has servants.

BONITA: Only one!

DULCE: That's one more than we have.

BONITA: You can have him. He watches me.

SOFIA: Ew!

BONITA: But I don't think he'd do anything. He's just painfully honest.

DULCE: It sounds kind of lonely, especially if you're still a virgin.

BONITA: I do miss you both. As irritating as you are.

SOFIA: By the way, how's Father's stick?

(Lighting change, and BONITA *is back in the* MASTEMA *house with* NICOLAS, *who is preparing for a trip.)*

BONITA: How long will you be in the city?

NICOLAS: Just overnight. Will you miss me?

BONITA: I will. Ratel is rather a cold comfort.

NICOLAS: He's rude.

BONITA: Yes! Can't you let him go?

NICOLAS: You'll get used to him.

BONITA: He just says what he thinks.

NICOLAS: Very reliable that way.

BONITA: He says he knows things about you.

NICOLAS: *(Chuckles)* Been with me a long time. He's harmless, really. *(Holds her)* I'll miss you, too.

BONITA: You've been very kind and patient.

NICOLAS: I'm nothing to be afraid of.

BONITA: It's not you. I'm afraid of own thoughts. They're unclean.

NICOLAS: I like unclean thoughts, especially about me.

(BONITA *moves away from* NICOLAS.)

BONITA: My sister's after me to open that silly cellar door.

NICOLAS: But you won't, will you?

BONITA: You're my husband. She's just my sister.

NICOLAS: I know I can trust you.

BONITA: It's a test! That's not very trusting.

(NICOLAS *looks alarmed.*)

BONITA: I can't imagine what would persuade me to open it. Dulce's the curious one.

NICOLAS: What's your sister think I've got down there? Money? Gold? Diamonds? (*Holds her again*) Aren't I treasure enough? You're certainly enough for me. Or you could be.

(BONITA *moves away from* NICOLAS *again, picks up the staff.*)

BONITA: What is it you'll be doing in the city?

NICOLAS: Legal affairs, very boring.

BONITA: I'm interested.

NICOLAS: Really? In tort law? Intellectual property rights?

BONITA: I thought you specialized in real estate.

NICOLAS: It all runs together, serious stuff sometimes, felonies, capital crimes.

BONITA: Capital crimes?!

NICOLAS: Don't worry, I'm just the lawyer.

BONITA: Can we throw this away?

NICOLAS: Why?

BONITA: It's a nasty old stick.

(NICOLAS *takes it away from* BONITA.)

BONITA: There's something on it. *(Wipes her hands)*

NICOLAS: Maybe I should put it in the basement, out of sight!

BONITA: It looks terrible, no matter where it is.

NICOLAS: It's antique.

BONITA: It's horrid. And this is my house, too, isn't it?

NICOLAS: On our wedding night you needed a bath. A very long bath. And then you didn't feel well for a few days. After that it was your period.

BONITA: It was!

NICOLAS: For how long?

BONITA: Most girls cycle with the moon—I cycle with Mars.

NICOLAS: And now. Unclean thoughts. *Thoughts?!*

BONITA: Thoughts can be more overwhelming than anything!

NICOLAS: What were your thoughts when you married me? Money? Security? Are you sure it's your sister who's after my treasure? I've given you everything you want, and what have you given me?

BONITA: All right, keep your damn stick!

NICOLAS: That's it! A little fire! A little passion! Now you're hot! Now you're melting! *(He grabs and kisses her roughly.)*

(BONITA *struggles.*)

BONITA: No! Please! I will! I will! But not this way!

NICOLAS: I've tried every which way!

(BONITA *breaks away from* NICOLAS, *runs, falls.*)

BONITA: Ratel! Help! Ratel!

NICOLAS: *(Picking up the staff)* He's old. And deaf.

(NICOLAS *raises the staff as* BONITA *cowers and screams. Thunder and lighting change. They disappear in darkness, and* DULCE *and* SOFIA *are revealed at their window with light streaming in and the sound of rain pouring.*)

SOFIA: How does it do that? The sun so bright, and the rain just pouring!

DULCE: It's not natural.

SOFIA: Our weather's gone insane.

DULCE: At least the drought seems to be over.

SOFIA: There should be a rainbow. The sun refracting through the giant prism of the storm. Where's the rainbow?

DULCE: Maybe—over there—is that—?

SOFIA: In the west?

DULCE: Yes.

SOFIA: Don't look directly at the sun!

DULCE: Is it? A rainbow? Do you see one?

SOFIA: No.

DULCE: Oh. I was hoping.

(Lights up on BONITA, *who shows evidence of a beating, a black eye or some other kind of bruise, perhaps torn clothing.* RATEL *stands before her.)*

BONITA: Can you tell me what's down there?

RATEL: I'm under orders not to.

BONITA: Can you tell me how to open it?

RATEL: It's not locked.

BONITA: Then what's inside must be of little worth.

RATEL: What you most desire lies behind that door.

BONITA: How do you know what I desire?

RATEL: You didn't want to get married but sacrificed everything for financial security.

BONITA: For my family, not just me!

RATEL: And yet, you want more.

BONITA: I'm not greedy!

RATEL: And he beat you.

BONITA: That doesn't mean I must break faith.

RATEL: Do as you choose. I've got to milk the cows.

(RATEL *leaves.* BONITA *stands there a moment, turns to look at the door.)*

DULCE: *(Appearing in light)* A forbidden cellar!? What's down there?

SOFIA: *(Appearing in light)* His wife before you? Or what's left of her?

BONITA: Ratel? Are you peeping through a spyhole?

RATEL: No!

BONITA: But you're listening!

RATEL: Moooo!

(Sound of a slamming door)

BONITA: Ratel?

SOFIA: I wonder if my stick's down there.

DULCE: It's half yours anyway, community property.

(Lights out on SOFIA *and* DULCE.*)*

BONITA: Ratel?

(Steeling herself, BONITA *goes to the door and opens it. The contents are only visible to her, but a golden light shines upon her from within.)*

BONITA: Oh! Gold! Walls of gold! And a golden staircase! Is it solid? *(Steps cautiously inside)* It is! Solid gold! All the way down! So shiny and steep! And no railing!

(BONITA disappears inside the door, her cautious footsteps on the gold staircase echoing as she descends. Suddenly the door slams shut behind her.)

BONITA: Ratel! *(From within)* Are you there?

(Sound of BONITA running back up the steps and pounding on the door.)

BONITA: Ratel! Ratel! Open the door! I'm locked in! There's no handle on this side! Help!

(Sound of BONITA slamming herself against the door.)

BONITA: Ratel! Let me out!

(Sound of BONITA slamming herself against the door.)

BONITA: I'll break it down if I have to—

(BONITA slams herself against the door a third time, but apparently loses her balance and falls. She screams.)

BONITA: Ratel!!

(The sound of BONITA's scream dies away as she falls very, very far. Lighting change reveals NICOLAS sitting with DULCE and SOFIA in their home. DULCE sobs into a handkerchief. SOFIA's tears are silent.)

SOFIA: She...fell?

NICOLAS: I should never have left her home alone.

SOFIA: Wasn't the servant there?

NICOLAS: He was doing chores outside. When he came back, he found her.

DULCE: Ohhh!

NICOLAS: She died instantly and without pain.

SOFIA: *(Wiping tears)* We'll bury her next to Father.

NICOLAS: I interred her right away in my family plot. This hot weather.

DULCE: Ohhh!

NICOLAS: Such beauty lost. Such goodness.

SOFIA: You could have sent for us!

NICOLAS: I wanted to tell you in person.

DULCE: That's very considerate.

SOFIA: Still, I don't understand—

NICOLAS: Perhaps, in my grief, I made the wrong choice. Forgive me.

DULCE: Of course!

NICOLAS: I feel responsible—I shouldn't have gone to the city—

DULCE: It was an accident!

NICOLAS: Legally I inherit the eleven thousand acres as community property, but because we were married so briefly, it hardly seems fair—

SOFIA: Yes, hardly fair—

NICOLAS: I'll destroy our agreement here in front of you— *(Pulls out the agreement)* So the land reverts to your family—

DULCE: Wait.

NICOLAS & SOFIA: What?

DULCE: The agreement requires you to marry a Ramirez sister and accept the land as dowry, yes?

NICOLAS: That's correct, but—

SOFIA: Dulce, our sister is dead—!

DULCE: I'm not dead! You're not dead!

SOFIA: Her body—although hastily buried—is probably still warm!

NICOLAS: Well, as I said, the weather—

DULCE: We can still fulfill the terms.

SOFIA: Who can?

DULCE: I realize I'm not as beautiful as Bonita, but I offer myself so you may keep the dowry.

(NICOLAS *and* SOFIA *look at each other in astonishment, then at* DULCE.)

SOFIA: Dulce!

NICOLAS: That's thoughtful and sweet of you, but—

SOFIA: Thoughtful? It's horrible!

DULCE: If I...marry Nick, the eleven thousand acres stay in the family and we're provided for— (*To* SOFIA) Otherwise, the two of us will starve to death on thirty-three thousand acres we can't afford to farm!

SOFIA: You'd be living in a house with significant safety concerns.

NICOLAS: I'm taking additional precautions.

SOFIA: You have no qualms? Not even the slightest discomfort? Your wife died two days ago and you're ready to take another?

NICOLAS: The marriage would resolve legal issues for all of us. And Dulce's offer—especially in these uncomfortable circumstances—is the soul of self-sacrificing sweetness.

SOFIA: Ah, yes, very true.

DULCE: Even if I had other choices, this is what I'd choose.

NICOLAS: (*Taking* DULCE's *hand*) I'm flattered.

SOFIA: I'm flabbergasted!

(*Lighting change puts* SOFIA *in the dark and* DULCE *and* NICOLAS *back at his home.*)

NICOLAS: I have you tell you your sister and I never—

DULCE: I know.

NICOLAS: She told you?

DULCE: We were very close. And I know how she is. Was.

NICOLAS: Afraid. Of me. Can you imagine? It broke my heart.

DULCE: I won't break your heart.

NICOLAS: You're not afraid.

DULCE: You're the one should be afraid.

(DULCE *jumps* NICOLAS, *amorously, bowling him over backwards as they both laugh. Lights up on* SOFIA *alone.* DULCE *and* NICOLAS *exhaust every sexual quirk, kink and position with great enthusiasm while* SOFIA *speaks the letter she is writing.*)

SOFIA: Dear Dulce: Warmest wishes on your wedding. I trust your wedding night was more enjoyable than poor Bonita's. I miss her terribly, and you, too! It's lonely here without anyone. I try to keep up the estate, but your husband hasn't sent the money he promised to hire more help. Could you speak to him about that? I admit to being a little worried for you. You are so easily swept off your feet, and I'll also admit he has his qualities, but the circumstances of Bonita's death...I'm naturally skeptical, as you know. Please answer as soon as you receive this. I'm not as busy as you, apparently, and you and Nick remain uppermost in my thoughts. Much love,
Sofia
P S. Have you seen my stick?

(*Lights out on* SOFIA *and up on a post-coital* NICOLAS [*exhausted*] *and* DULCE [*rarin' to go*].)

NICOLAS: That was...comprehensive.

DULCE: Oh, no, much more to come! *(Reaches for him)*

NICOLAS: *(Avoiding her)* No more to come for at least a few hours!

DULCE: *(Pulling herself together)* Would you like some oysters?

NICOLAS: Just a little rest. You seem very—please don't take this the wrong way—expert.

DULCE: Just enthusiastic!

NICOLAS: You don't mean to say you've never—?

DULCE: Sofia's not the only one who reads books.

NICOLAS: But—that thing with the—eggplant...?

DULCE: I have wide-ranging taste in literature.

(Lights out on NICOLAS and up on SOFIA with DULCE.)

SOFIA: Surely he's not that naive!

DULCE: He's relieved. Bonita—

SOFIA & DULCE: God rest her soul.

DULCE: —Apparently starved the man, and I offer—

SOFIA: A banquet. Please don't give me any details about the eggplant.

DULCE: We ate it after.

(SOFIA rolls her eyes)

DULCE: He likes my cooking, too! I'm giving him what he wants, which makes us both happy. He delights in everything a body can experience, all the senses.

SOFIA: Sounds like a good match.

DULCE: Good indeed! I've never been so—satisfied!

SOFIA: I don't want to hear!   DULCE: He's almost
                                 disproportionate! Big
                                 and cold—!

SOFIA: Cold?

DULCE: Which is perfect because I'm so—you know—hot—down there.

SOFIA: Enough!

DULCE: Are you all right?

SOFIA: Just a little over-informed.

DULCE: When you wrote me you sounded forlorn.

SOFIA: I have plenty to do. By the way, have you opened the forbidden door you were so curious about?

DULCE: I haven't had a moment to think about it! Between cooking and...*cooking*...

SOFIA: Do you two have actual conversations?

(*Lighting puts* SOFIA *in darkness and reveals* NICOLAS *preparing for a trip.*)

DULCE: Must you go?

NICOLAS: It's a very important matter.

DULCE: What's more important than us?

NICOLAS: A war.

DULCE: A war? You're an attorney!

NICOLAS: A small war, but a war nonetheless.

DULCE: (*Sidles up to him*) Is your little war more important than—? Smell.

NICOLAS: (*Sniffs her*) Is that cinnamon? Nutmeg?

DULCE: And ginger and clove. I'm your little pumpkin pie.

NICOLAS: Wish I had time for dessert.

DULCE: Not even a taste?

NICOLAS: Governments are falling.

DULCE: Small ones. How can you leave me unsatisfied?

NICOLAS: Have some pie.

DULCE: I'm not really in the mood for anything sweet.

NICOLAS: I have to go.

DULCE: *(Hands him the staff)* I'm in the mood for rough.

NICOLAS: Where'd you find that?

DULCE: If it's so precious, why do you leave it lying around? It gives me ideas. *(She shows him her bare back)*

NICOLAS: I haven't the time.

DULCE: Try it. I don't want you to get bored.

NICOLAS: I'm not bored! I have a war!

DULCE: Then one skirmish before you go. A warm up.

(NICOLAS hesitates.)

DULCE: I want *all* your love.

NICOLAS: Even if it hurts?

DULCE: Especially. Otherwise, how do you know it's real?

NICOLAS: Very well. *(Raises the staff)* But just one—

DULCE: Make it good.

(Lights out on them and up on SOFIA looking out the window. Sound of a thwack and a moan of pleasure from DULCE, instantly followed by lightning and a crack of thunder. Rain pours down outside the window, but bright sunlight streams in.)

SOFIA: *(Writing)*
Dear Dulce:
Forgive me for worrying, but I haven't heard from you in weeks. Haven't you exhausted him yet? Have you peeked in the forbidden cellar? And what of my stick? If he's not using it, I'd like it back. I can't wait much longer for your husband to send money, so I'm trying to rent 10,000 acres to the Espositos. The sticking point

is water rights, of course. By the way, it's raining again, the sun is shining, and no rainbow. It's just not normal!

(Lighting change puts SOFIA *in the dark and reveals* DULCE, *only slightly worse for wear, with* RATEL.*)*

DULCE: Ratel, darling, how long have you worked for my husband?

RATEL: Too long.

DULCE: Your loyalty is astonishing, but you don't seem exactly happy in your employment. Is there anything I can do?

RATEL: I doubt it. The master's set in his ways.

DULCE: What would you say is your greatest skill?

RATEL: Are you interviewing me for a different position, mistress?

DULCE: Oh, Heavens no! I've just observed that you're very honest. You tell the unvarnished truth, no matter how unpleasant. You don't give a shit.

RATEL: Is this an attempt at flattery?

DULCE: I'm just being honest. Like you. Have you ever told a lie in your life? Even one?

RATEL: No.

DULCE: Of course, if you were a normal person, that would be a lie right there. But you're not a normal person, are you, Ratel?

RATEL: No.

DULCE: So if I ask you a question about the cellar, you'd have to tell the truth?

RATEL: Yes.

DULCE: I'd have to ask it precisely, because you could be truthful but misleading if my question is too ambiguous.

(RATEL *doesn't answer.*)

DULCE: That was a question.

RATEL: Yes.

DULCE: What's inside?

RATEL: That which you most desire.

DULCE: Apparently I was imprecise.

RATEL: What is it you desire?

DULCE: What do you think I desire?

RATEL: That would be an opinion.

DULCE: I am requesting your honest opinion.

RATEL: Flesh.

DULCE: Go on.

RATEL: You crave experiences that stimulate the five senses, you embrace sensation, even pain. You embrace embraces.

DULCE: Honest and observant. No wonder Nick's kept you so long. If I open that door, will you tell my husband?

RATEL: No.

DULCE: And how do I open it?

RATEL: Since your sister's accident, the door has been locked. I cannot give you the key.

DULCE: Bonita died in there?

RATEL: Yes.

DULCE: Why didn't you tell me earlier?

RATEL: You didn't ask.

DULCE: Ah. Nick said she fell.

RATEL: Down the cellar stairs.

DULCE: Where do you keep the key?

(RATEL *hesitates.*)

DULCE: Where is the key, my honest friend?

RATEL: On a chain around my neck.

DULCE: Oh. Here? *(Reaches into his shirt)* Yes, there it is. I know you can't give it to me, but someday I may just take it.

RATEL: *(Stepping away from her)* I'm a weak old man, powerless to stop you.

(Lighting change puts DULCE with SOFIA.)

SOFIA: Oh! I'm so glad to see you!

DULCE: Me, too! You'll have to come visit.

SOFIA: Not with that creepy old servant.

DULCE: He always tells the truth—you just have to ask the right questions. He said Bonita fell down the basement stairs!

SOFIA: Don't go in there!

(Lighting change puts SOFIA in the dark and DULCE back in the MASTEMA home by herself. She pulls out a key, contemplates it, then unlocks the forbidden door and throws it open. She gasps with delight at what she sees as she is flooded in undulating pink and red light.)

MALE VOICE: Dulce!

ANOTHER MALE VOICE: Pretty Dulce!

YET ANOTHER MALE VOICE: Sweet Dulce.

(DULCE peers inside cautiously.)

DULCE: Who are you? *(She walks carefully through the door, slowly advancing down the stairs.)*

MALE VOICE: Welcome, Dulce, come see what I've got.

ANOTHER MALE VOICE: No, come to me!

YET ANOTHER MALE VOICE: We can share. Dulce likes to share.

DULCE: *(Off)* Yes. Oh, yes!

(Suddenly NICOLAS appears with his staff and slams the door shut behind DULCE.)

DULCE: Ratel? Is that you?

NICOLAS: It's Nicolas!

(Sound of her running up the stairs.)

DULCE: Oh, my darling, open the door!

NICOLAS: You were forbidden to open it. But you gave in to temptation. I'm disappointed.

DULCE: I'm sorry, sweetheart! Nothing happened!

NICOLAS: Nothing?

MALE VOICES: Nothing? *(They laugh.)*

DULCE: Forgive me, dear! Don't leave me here with these strange—albeit quite handsome—men!

MALE VOICES: You're stuck with us! Forever! Let us love you, Dulce. Pretty Dulce! Sweet Dulce!

DULCE: Help, Nick! Let me out! Please, darling! Stop it! Oh, that's enough! Don't! I don't mind a little pain, but—ow! Nicolas!

(His back to the door, NICOLAS listens as the VOICES grow more insistent and DULCE becomes more panicked. He smiles.)

MALE VOICES: Just a little lick! A bite! A tiny taste of your sweetness! A nip! A nibble! Delicious!

DULCE: Nicolas, they're too much! They want too much! Make them stop! You're hurting me! Open the door! Have mercy!

(DULCE *screams as darkness falls suddenly and* NICOLAS
is illuminated by lightning. Lighting change puts NICOLAS
back in the Ramirez home with SOFIA.)

SOFIA: She ran away?

NICOLAS: Not...by herself.

SOFIA: With...a man?

NICOLAS: More than one, actually.

SOFIA: She was kidnapped! Raped!

(NICOLAS *just looks at* SOFIA.)

SOFIA: Surely she didn't go voluntarily.

(NICOLAS *just looks at* SOFIA.)

SOFIA: You've rather bad luck with wives.

NICOLAS: I've divorced her.

SOFIA: Already?

NICOLAS: Marital fidelity is part of the contract. She's in
violation. It's automatic.

SOFIA: Why haven't I heard from her?

NICOLAS: I expect she'll be in touch when she and her
lover—excuse me, *lovers*—settle down.

SOFIA: Who are they?

NICOLAS: Undesirable types. I can't even think about
them—it pains my heart.

SOFIA: I have to find her!

NICOLAS: She'll turn up. Eventually.

SOFIA: Alive, I hope!

NICOLAS: Unless...

SOFIA: What?

NICOLAS: She has some extreme tastes in...well, it
was fun at first, but she took it farther than even I was

comfortable. And these men seem more extreme than she.

SOFIA: So you fear for her safety!

NICOLAS: Yes, but I have my people working on it. They're doing all they can to make sure no further harm comes to her.

SOFIA: Further?!

NICOLAS: The greatest harm is to her reputation, which is her own responsibility.

SOFIA: You seem remarkably calm for having lost two wives in the space of a few weeks.

NICOLAS: If I give in to my emotions I suspect I will be done for.

SOFIA: I'm done for! I've lost two sisters! They're all the family I have!

NICOLAS: You have me.

SOFIA: You're not blood. A brother-in-law. Twice. And now an ex-brother-in-law.

NICOLAS: Unless…

SOFIA: What?

NICOLAS: We still have a contract.

SOFIA: Third time's the charm? I don't think so.

NICOLAS: It's actually stipulated.

SOFIA: That I have to marry you?

NICOLAS: As long as there is a Ramirez sister eligible.

SOFIA: You've rather a poor track record with Ramirez sisters.

NICOLAS: I have a confession.

SOFIA: You killed them!

NICOLAS: Bonita fell! Dulce ran off!

SOFIA: What are you confessing, then?

NICOLAS: You're the Ramirez sister I wanted all along.

SOFIA: Why? I'm neither beautiful like Bonita nor sweet like Dulce.

NICOLAS: Beauty fades and sweetness cloys.

SOFIA: You didn't love them?

NICOLAS: Marriage is but a legal arrangement.

SOFIA: And you're a lawyer.

NICOLAS: You're clever and you know how to use a stick to best advantage.

SOFIA: I know how to fight?

NICOLAS: For justice and truth.

SOFIA: How is my stick?

NICOLAS: It misses you.

SOFIA: You've a most peculiar way of courting. How could I possibly contemplate this kind of—union— under these sudden and devastating circumstances?

NICOLAS: You love me.

SOFIA: My sisters didn't?

NICOLAS: Bonita loved my money—that was clear. Dulce loved my…looks, I guess.

SOFIA: How could I love you? We hardly know each other.

NICOLAS: I notice you haven't denied it.

(*Lighting change puts* NICOLAS *in darkness as* SOFIA *puts on wedding attire.* BONITA *and* DULCE *appear isolated in light but don't help dress her, as they are dead. They look it.*)

BONITA: The house is very nice, a lot like ours in fact, but very isolated.

DULCE: I'm giving him what he wants, which makes us both happy.

BONITA: He's very understanding and patient.

DULCE: He delights in everything a body can experience, all the senses.

(SOFIA *finishes dressing, steels herself. Lighting change puts her sisters in darkness and* SOFIA *in the* MASTEMA *home with* NICOLAS.)

NICOLAS: (*Caressing her*) Do you have everything you desire?

SOFIA: I don't know yet.

NICOLAS: I have everything I desire. And what's mine is yours.

SOFIA: I'd like to trust you.

NICOLAS: Do you feel I've been untruthful?

SOFIA: I miss my sisters.

NICOLAS: I have a confession.

SOFIA: Another one?

NICOLAS: Truth is the best way to start a marriage.

SOFIA: Also the best way to end one.

NICOLAS: You deserve the truth.

(*She steels herself*)

I'm not just an attorney.

SOFIA: What's worse than that?

NICOLAS: I thought perhaps you'd figured it out, guessed my name.

SOFIA: It's not Nicolas Mastema?

NICOLAS: Only a few know me by that one.

(SOFIA *shrugs.*)

NICOLAS: I'm the Devil.

SOFIA: That's what Dulce said.

NICOLAS: I don't mean in bed.

SOFIA: You're the King of Hell, the Great Satan, Lucifer?

NICOLAS: Those are some of my titles, yes.

SOFIA: So you have—what?—demons working for you? That must be an administrative nightmare.

NICOLAS: They do what I say.

SOFIA: They're your slaves?

NICOLAS: Where but Hell can a demon find work?

SOFIA: Is that where you go on your frequent business trips?

NICOLAS: My business is in the world.

SOFIA: Crime? War? Natural disasters?

NICOLAS: I keep busy.

SOFIA: Do you ever go to Hell?

NICOLAS: I prefer pleasant places.

SOFIA: Where are the horns, the tail, the cloven hooves?

NICOLAS: Old wives tales.

SOFIA: If you're the Devil, wouldn't you have the power to prevent Bonita from falling and Dulce from running off?

NICOLAS: *(Shrugs)* Free will.

SOFIA: I have a confession, too.

NICOLAS: Then we'll be even.

SOFIA: I don't believe in you.

NICOLAS: I'm your husband.

SOFIA: Which would make me—what?—the Devil's wife?

NICOLAS: Yes.

SOFIA: I believe in neither God nor the Devil. They're old-fashioned anthropomorphic ways to explain good and evil.

NICOLAS: I'm just…a metaphor?

SOFIA: Invented by religion to frighten children and ignorant folks into obedience.

NICOLAS: You think I'm lying.

SOFIA: Isn't that another of your titles, Prince of Lies?

NICOLAS: Sometimes the best lie is to tell the truth.

SOFIA: Kiss me. Unless your lips will send me straight to perdition.

NICOLAS: Don't say I never warned you.

(They kiss. BONITA and DULCE appear in separate lights as NICOLAS and SOFIA disappear in darkness. BONITA and DULCE look even worse.)

DULCE: I've never been so satisfied! He's almost disproportionate!

BONITA: He's hardly around. Just me and that servant. And the forbidden door.

(Lights out on DULCE and BONITA. All is darkness except for golden light seeping out from behind the forbidden door, accompanied after a moment by the sound of clinking gold. The light becomes rosy, followed by the sensual murmurs of many men. Finally a blue light emanates from the door briefly before the lights come up on SOFIA alone, no longer in wedding attire. She turns to look at the door, which looks quite ordinary, no light emanating from behind it. She looks around, sees no one, then approaches the door and rattles the

knob. It's locked. In shaking the door she dislodges the staff,
which falls out of a niche. She picks it up. RATEL *comes in.)*

RATEL: Don't touch that!

SOFIA: I gave it to your master as a wedding present.
It's community property now.

RATEL: True, but you don't know how to use it.

SOFIA: Is it dangerous?

RATEL: It has great power.

SOFIA: I know! *(Demonstrates martial arts moves)*

RATEL: Be careful!

SOFIA: What kind of power?

*(*RATEL *hesitates.)*

SOFIA: Dulce said you must always tell the truth.

RATEL: It can part the sea.

SOFIA: Uh-huh.

RATEL: If you hang a bronze serpent on it, it will cure
snakebite.

SOFIA: I'll keep that in mind.

RATEL: If you hang a man upon it, it can save the
world.

SOFIA: Anything else?

RATEL: Everything else.

SOFIA: Like a magic wand?

RATEL: You can't diminish it by belittling.

SOFIA: Does it have a name?

RATEL: Yes.

SOFIA: And that is?

RATEL: Faith.

SOFIA: A stick named Faith?

RATEL: Sort of.

SOFIA: Don't obfuscate with truth.

RATEL: Faith is what gives it power.

SOFIA: So it's just an ordinary stick invested with power by the belief of whomever wields it.

RATEL: Exactly.

SOFIA: And if you don't believe?

RATEL: It's just a stick.

SOFIA: Then in my skeptical hands, it's a dirty old stick—what's this on it?

RATEL: Are you asking me?

SOFIA: Yes.

RATEL: Blood.

SOFIA: *(Wiping her hands)* Whose?

RATEL: Women.

SOFIA: Which women...wives?

(RATEL nods.)

SOFIA: Is it my sisters' blood? Did Nick beat them with it?

RATEL: Yes.

SOFIA: On sunny days when the rain fell?

RATEL: The rain was their tears.

SOFIA: *(Skeptical)* Right. And how many wives has he had?

RATEL: *(Shrugs)* It rains a lot.

SOFIA: Did he kill them?

RATEL: No.

SOFIA: I'm serious now.

RATEL: I cannot lie.

SOFIA: He didn't kill them…but are they dead?

RATEL: Yes.

SOFIA: You say you always tell the truth, but how do I know that's not a lie?

RATEL: You can only believe.

SOFIA: I can't just—believe—without evidence. Did my sisters go through that door?

RATEL: Yes.

SOFIA: Are they there now?

RATEL: Yes. If you want evidence, take a look.

SOFIA: I'm living in a house with my sisters' bodies rotting in the basement?

RATEL: It's not a basement.

SOFIA: What is it?

(RATEL *hesitates*.)

SOFIA: The truth!

RATEL: Is truth your heart's desire?

SOFIA: Yes! What's beyond that door?

RATEL: Hell.

SOFIA: You'd think my husband would have said something.

RATEL: Perhaps he didn't wish to tempt you.

SOFIA: *(Laughs)* You're most certainly a liar. There's no Hell! Nor Heaven, nor the Devil, nor God! Even if my husband tells me he's the Prince of Darkness and you say Hades is our root cellar!

RATEL: *(Shrugs)* You asked.

SOFIA: Who has the key?

(RATEL *shows* SOFIA *the key.*)

SOFIA: Give it to me.

RATEL: I'm not allowed.

SOFIA: Bonita was right—you are frustratingly impertinent. *(She grabs the key and heads toward the door, then stops.)* Is this exactly what my sisters did, open this door and get sucked into a mythical dimension of everlasting torment?

RATEL: They entered of their own free will.

SOFIA: What did they see that lured them in?

RATEL: Their heart's desire.

SOFIA: They fell for a lie?

RATEL: Not a lie. They got their heart's desire.

SOFIA: Is there no way out for them?

RATEL: They're dead. They cannot change.

SOFIA: But there are lots of stories of people going to Hell and coming back out—

RATEL: Folk tales, fables—   SOFIA: Resurrecting—

RATEL: You can write anything in a book.

SOFIA: Could I look without going inside?

RATEL: Once you see their torment, you won't rush in to save them?

SOFIA: Not if I can't get out again.

RATEL: If you're that cold-blooded, go ahead. Of your own free will.

SOFIA: Nick may be afraid to fire you, but I'm not. I'm just saying.

(SOFIA unlocks the door and throws it open. Golden and rosy lights emanate. The voices BONITA and DULCE can be heard, but they are not visible. Whenever BONITA speaks, the light is golden, and when DULCE speaks, the light is rosy. SOFIA stares in horror at what she sees.)

BONITA & DULCE: *(Wailing)* Sofia!

SOFIA: Bonita! Dulce! What's happened to you?!

BONITA: He tricked us!

DULCE: When he was tired of us! *(Moans)*

BONITA: Said "Don't open that door—"

DULCE: So of course we did!

BONITA: How did he tempt you to open it?

SOFIA: He didn't. He never mentioned it.

DULCE: He will! He's the Devil! *(Moans)*

SOFIA: That's what he said, but he was joking.

BONITA: We're not joking!

SOFIA: Why are you moaning? Are you in pain?

DULCE: We're in Hell! *(Moans)*

SOFIA: *(Steps toward them)* Nonsense! You're in the cellar and I'll get you out of there!

BONITA & DULCE: Noooo!

(SOFIA stops at the threshold.)

DULCE: Once you step in, you can never get out!

BONITA: You can't save us. But save yourself!

DULCE: And punish him! *(Moans)*

SOFIA: If he's the Prince of All Evil, how can I punish him?

BONITA: Trick him into Hell!

DULCE: We'll take it from there!

SOFIA: Not that I believe you, but if he's the Devil, can't he go in and out of Hell as he pleases?

BONITA: Not without that staff.

SOFIA: *(Holding up the staff)* This stupid stick?

DULCE: He clutches it—!

BONITA: Holds it tight!   DULCE: Whenever he
                               comes in—

BONITA: It gives him the power to pass through Hell
safely.

SOFIA: *(To* RATEL*)* The power of Faith? My atheist
father won *Faith* from the Devil in a bet?

(RATEL *nods.*)

SOFIA: So if I carried this with me, could I go in the
basement, get my sisters, and bring them out again?

BONITA: It's too late for us!   DULCE: It's not a
                                   basement!

SOFIA: Could I?

RATEL: No one's ever gone in and out before.

SOFIA: Except Nick.

DULCE: But you can trick him! *(Moans)*

(RATEL *disappears.*)

SOFIA: How can I talk him into entering Hell with me?
Ask for a guided tour?

DULCE: You'll think of something.

BONITA: You're the clever one.

SOFIA: Not clever enough to trick the Devil! I can't lie to
him.

BONITA: Then use the truth!

DULCE: Every man has a little handle you can use to
control him. What's his?

BONITA: What does he want from you?

SOFIA: I don't know. Love?

BONITA & DULCE: Love!

DULCE: Go! Find him!

BONITA: Close the door before he suspects!

DULCE: Close it!

SOFIA: This is ridiculous. I can't leave you in there!

BONITA: Trust me, we'll be no worse off than we are right now.

DULCE: And we'll be avenged! *(Moans)*

BONITA: We'll be right here.

DULCE: We're always here.

BONITA & DULCE: We love you! Close the door!

SOFIA: I love you, too! *(She slams the door shut and turns to RATEL but he's gone.)*

SOFIA: Ratel?

NICOLAS: *(Appears)* What are you doing with my staff?

SOFIA: Oh, Nick! Welcome home!

NICOLAS: Here, let me take that.

SOFIA: Did you kill my father to get this back?

NICOLAS: You said he had a heart attack.

SOFIA: He handed it to me when he was dying!   NICOLAS: Which was God's will.

SOFIA: So this is mine as much as yours, isn't it?

NICOLAS: *(Shrugs)* As you wish.

SOFIA: Speaking of which, Mefistofeles...?

NICOLAS: It rather suits me that you don't believe. But at least I told you the truth.

SOFIA: You can prove it to me.

NICOLAS: How?

SOFIA: If you're the Devil, then you own Hell.

NICOLAS: It's not exactly real estate.

SOFIA: Through the community property clause in the dowry agreement, I'm half owner. Of Hell.

NICOLAS: You're being silly.

SOFIA: Husbands always say that when their wives are right.

NICOLAS: You believe in neither the Devil nor Hell.

SOFIA: Change my mind—take me there.

NICOLAS: It's not tourist-friendly. You kind of have to be dead.

SOFIA: What about Virgil?

NICOLAS: You can write anything in a book.

SOFIA: If you truly loved me, you'd take me to Hell.

NICOLAS: You won't like what you see.

SOFIA: If you do, I'll tell you I love you.

NICOLAS: That's my heart's desire. You realize a promise to the Devil is ironclad on both sides.

SOFIA: Of course. You're an attorney. How soon can we go? Do we need protective clothing of any kind?

NICOLAS: People go to Hell all the time with no preparation whatsoever.

SOFIA: But they can't get out.

NICOLAS: You must hold onto this staff the entire time. If you let go, you won't get out either. We can go now if you wish.

SOFIA: Is love truly your heart's desire?

NICOLAS: I've never known what it feels like to be loved for who I am.

(NICOLAS *holds out the staff.* SOFIA *grabs a hold.*)

SOFIA: It's a deal. Shall I ask Ratel to arrange transportation?

NICOLAS: Not necessary. It's right through that door.

SOFIA: Convenient! *(Reaches for door)* May I?

NICOLAS: But don't let go of the staff!

(SOFIA opens the door. Multicolored lights play on them as they peer through the doorway.)

NICOLAS: Now do you believe?

SOFIA: It doesn't look especially awful.

NICOLAS: One last chance.

SOFIA: As the Devil's wife, I'm half owner, and it would be immoral of me to be an absentee landlord.

(They disappear through the doorway. Instant lighting change turns the MASTEMA house into Hell and reveals BONITA wearing a long gold dress, perhaps a continuation of the gold walls and floor. She looks dead, exhausted and hollow-eyed. SOFIA and NICOLAS [holding the staff] appear.)

SOFIA: Bonita! I thought you were dead!

BONITA: I am.

NICOLAS: She fell.

BONITA: Into Hell! My husband's servant—your husband's servant—told me I'd find my heart's desire. Hello, Nicolas.

NICOLAS: Bonita, you're wearing your heart's desire, just as he said. Security, forever.

BONITA: Gold! This dress is pure gold!

SOFIA: So you're not...suffering?

BONITA: I've no physical discomfort. *(She tries to move but can't get very far)* But gold is heavy, and I can't take this off.

SOFIA: It's beautiful.

BONITA: I'm perfectly comfortable, my desire satisfied for all time.

NICOLAS: This is what you wished for.

BONITA: And it's Hell!

(BONITA *lunges for* NICOLAS, *almost reaching him, but is held back by the dress as he dodges her.*)

NICOLAS: Beware your heart's desire! It will trap you!

BONITA: (*Still reaching for* NICOLAS) A little late now, my love!

(*As* NICOLAS *and* SOFIA *back away from* BONITA, *lighting reveals* DULCE *scantily dressed and looking worn out. She moans and lunges for* NICOLAS, *barely missing him as he dodges.*)

DULCE: My love!

SOFIA: Dulce!

MALE VOICES: Dulce! My love! Let me touch you! I feel you!

SOFIA: What's happening to you?

DULCE: Pleasure! (*Moans*) Constant pleasure!

MALE VOICES: So soft! So warm! So loving!

SOFIA: Who are those voices? I don't see anyone!

DULCE: Ask him! Ask our husband!

SOFIA: Nick, who are they?

DULCE: Demons!

NICOLAS: Yes, they're demons.

MALE VOICES: So pretty, so loving!	DULCE: So handsome, so loving!

SOFIA: Are they…making love to you?

DULCE: (*Writhing*) All the time! Their hands, their tongues, every part of them!

SOFIA: So you're not suffering either?

DULCE: It's ecstasy—eternally!

SOFIA: Your heart's desire!

DULCE: Without a break!

SOFIA: Pleasure is Hell?

DULCE: Anything can be Hell—!

BONITA: —If it never ends!

DULCE: Pleasure!

BONITA: Gold!

DULCE: Torture!   BONITA: Torment!

SOFIA: This is a truly terrible place! Why did you bring me here?

NICOLAS: You wanted to come. You wanted the truth.

SOFIA: Why was Hell even created?

NICOLAS: So people could have their heart's desire.

DULCE: *(Grabbing* NICOLAS*)* You're my heart's desire!

NICOLAS: *(Trying to pull away)* You only want pleasure!

BONITA: *(Grabbing* NICOLAS*)* You're my heart's desire!

NICOLAS: You only want gold! Let go!

SOFIA: They love you, Nick! Isn't that what you want most? To be truly loved for who you are?

BONITA: The Devil wants to be loved?

DULCE: We'll give you love!

SOFIA: You have your heart's desire!

NICOLAS: I want to be loved by you! Their grip is like iron!

BONITA: It's a death grip!

DULCE: The power of death!

NICOLAS: *(Struggling)* They won't let go! Beat them, Sofia!

SOFIA: I can't beat my own sisters!

DULCE: He beat us!

NICOLAS: Only because you wanted it!

BONITA: I didn't want it!

NICOLAS: You'll have to beat them or we'll be trapped here!

SOFIA: What can I beat them with?

NICOLAS: I can't let go of the staff—it's our safe passage out of Hell.

SOFIA: If you let me take it, I'll give you your heart's desire.

NICOLAS: You'll tell me you love me?

SOFIA: Better than that. I will actually love you.

NICOLAS: I'm trusting you.

(NICOLAS *lets the staff go.* SOFIA *lifts it.* BONITA *and* DULCE *scream, fearing she'll beat them.*)

SOFIA: Step aside, sisters—this isn't for you.

NICOLAS: But you love me!

SOFIA: Is love more important than truth?

NICOLAS: I love you!

SOFIA: I can't beat anyone. (*Lowering the staff*) I have to go.

NICOLAS: You can't escape Hell without me.

SOFIA: (*Indicates staff*) I have Faith.

NICOLAS: Bargains with the Devil are ironclad!

SOFIA: On both sides! What was Father's bet with you? How did he win this?

BONITA: Go, Sofia! It's too late for us!

DULCE: We'll hold him! Go!

NICOLAS: You said you'd say it! You can't go back on your word!

SOFIA: I do love you. With all my heart, not just words. Despite who you are, despite this terrible place, despite the eternal damnation you prepared for my sisters, I love you in the way you wish to be loved.

NICOLAS: So you can't leave me.

(NICOLAS *reaches for the staff, almost gets it, but* SOFIA *pulls it away.*)

DULCE & BONITA: Sofia, go, before he tricks you like he tricked us!

SOFIA: My love is your heart's desire—and your Hell. But I'm leaving you here. That's mine.

NICOLAS: You're my wife!

SOFIA: Yes, I'll always be the Devil's wife.

(*A clap of thunder. Lightning flashes, and an instant lighting change leaves* NICOLAS, BONITA *and* DULCE *in the dark and puts* SOFIA *back in the* MASTEMA *home. She bursts into tears while still holding the staff. After a moment* RATEL *appears.*)

RATEL: Mistress, do you require anything?

SOFIA: Yes, Ratel, actually I am in great need. I require what only you can give: the truth.

RATEL: About?

SOFIA: Hell. I...lost Nick there.

RATEL: My condolences. I see your heart is breaking.

SOFIA: As his widow am I now the sole owner of Hell?

RATEL: Yes. You are officially Queen of Hell.

SOFIA: Queen! Of such a vile place! Can I get rid of it?

RATEL: It's full of people! Where would they go?

SOFIA: How many exactly?

RATEL: Ninety-nine billion, four hundred thirty-eight million, seven hundred ninety-two thousand, five hundred and six.

SOFIA: That must be everyone who's ever lived.

RATEL: They all got their heart's desire.

SOFIA: So there's room in Heaven?

RATEL: Room in Heaven? For sinners?

SOFIA: As Queen of Hell, I'll negotiate that with my counterpart.

RATEL: The...King of Heaven?

SOFIA: Yes.

RATEL: You mean God? You don't believe in him.

SOFIA: That was before I went to Hell.

RATEL: Where you found faith.

SOFIA: Yes, against my better judgment, against all reason! I believe in God. Remarkable! Can you arrange an audience?

RATEL: It's difficult.

SOFIA: Don't try to protect me. I've just escaped the Devil. Isn't God supposed to be benevolent?

RATEL: God is good, yes.

SOFIA: So why does he even permit Nicolas to exist? Why should there be evil?

RATEL: God only knows.

SOFIA: *(Indicates staff)* Do I need to use this for safe passage to Heaven?

RATEL: No. He'll come here.

SOFIA: When?

RATEL: *(After a moment)* Now.

(SOFIA *looks around the room, sees no one else.*)

SOFIA: He's invisible?

RATEL: Not at the moment.

SOFIA: Oh. He's you.

RATEL: Yes.

SOFIA: You're God.

RATEL: That's right.

SOFIA: Serving the Devil.

RATEL: It's complicated.

SOFIA: Tell the truth.

RATEL: It was a way to you.

SOFIA: To me?

RATEL: You are my heart's desire.

SOFIA: Why me?

RATEL: You know how to use a stick to best advantage.

SOFIA: *(Indicating staff)* You mean—Faith? I don't believe in anything!

RATEL: Your skepticism made you intriguing, a challenge. But now you believe—you just said so. And you love me.

SOFIA: How can I love you when I've only just now found out who you are?

RATEL: You told me you love me.

SOFIA: When? Where?

RATEL: In Hell. *(He removes his white beard and wig, changes his posture, and reveals that he's NICOLAS.)*

SOFIA: Nicolas. How'd you get out of Hell?

NICOLAS: I'm God.

SOFIA: And the Devil?

NICOLAS: Now do you understand?

SOFIA: So…God is good, but sometimes wants to instigate crimes, start a war, condemn ninety— nine billion souls to Hell?

NICOLAS: Without bad, no one would appreciate the good. *(Reaches for staff)* Why don't you give me that?

SOFIA: *(Keeping the staff)* So you became the Devil to make the world love God?

NICOLAS: Love: my heart's desire.

SOFIA: Then give me my heart's desire.

NICOLAS: Truth? First give me that.

(NICOLAS *reaches for staff,* SOFIA *pulls it away.)*

SOFIA: I've given up on truth. I want compassion— relief for my sisters and all those souls suffering in Hell!

NICOLAS: What you think of as Heaven doesn't exist.

SOFIA: How can there be Hell without Heaven? What about balance?

NICOLAS: I give them their heart's desire forever. Isn't that Heaven?

SOFIA: Heaven and Hell are the same?

NICOLAS: That's fair isn't it? That's compassionate. *(Reaches for staff)*

SOFIA: *(Keeping it from him)* Why do you want this so bad?

NICOLAS: Faith is a form of love.

SOFIA: And power. God's only power comes from faith!

NICOLAS: Yes. That's the great truth.

SOFIA: You want love. Worship! That's pathetic!

NICOLAS: It's all anybody wants.

SOFIA: Then I hold in my hand all your power.

NICOLAS: But you don't know how to use it.

SOFIA: Oh, yes, I do! *(She whacks him with the staff.)* *(Thunder)*

NICOLAS: What was that for?

SOFIA: For your truth disguised as lies! *(Whacks)*

NICOLAS: You can't just...beat me!

SOFIA: Faith is the only way to beat God—or the Devil!

(SOFIA whacks NICOLAS again. Thunder with every blow)

NICOLAS: You're my wife!

SOFIA: So you should beat me, like all your other wives? *(Whacks)* Like my sisters! *(Whacks)* That's for them! *(Whacks)* That's for the ninety-nine billion!

NICOLAS: Stop it, Sofia! That hurts!

SOFIA: No one's ever beaten you before?

NICOLAS: Only your father!

SOFIA: He beat you?

NICOLAS: In debate! Our bet!

SOFIA: How'd he beat you?

NICOLAS: He bet he could prove I didn't exist.

SOFIA: So you gave him a heart attack! This is for Father! *(Whacks)* That's for capital crimes! *(Whacks)* For the wars!

NICOLAS: Ow! *(Falls)*

SOFIA: The floods! *(Whacks)* The droughts! *(Whacks)* The locusts! *(Whacks)* The lawyers!

(It begins to rain, but the sun also shines. Perhaps some lightning. SOFIA begins to cry furious tears of anger and sadness.)

NICOLAS: I think you broke a rib! You can't do this!

SOFIA: I can't? What about free will?

NICOLAS: I'm bleeding!

SOFIA: Oh, I know how to use this, all right! *(Whacks)* You've used faith against us since the dawn of time! *(Whacks)*

NICOLAS: You're trying to kill me!

SOFIA: As only a believer can! And I'll inherit your kingdom—not just Hell but the world! *(Whacks)* Fix every injustice, right every wrong—!

NICOLAS: You'll do better than me?

SOFIA: I couldn't do worse!

NICOLAS: It's a terrible responsibility! You don't know what it means!

SOFIA: *(Whacks)* It means the end of the Devil! The end of evil! Saving the world!

NICOLAS: It's not that simple!

SOFIA: *(Whacks)* We should have tried this long ago! We'll be free!

NICOLAS: You can't kill God!

SOFIA: Yes, I can! You're only a metaphor!

(Several whacks. NICOLAS can hardly move. Perhaps blood spatters. A rainbow starts to appear.)

SOFIA: How'd my father win your debate?

NICOLAS: By...proving I don't exist.

SOFIA: How'd he do that?

NICOLAS: By not believing.

SOFIA: So you showed him no mercy! *(Whacks)*

NICOLAS: If you kill me, you'll become me!

SOFIA: I'll become God? *(Whacks)*

NICOLAS: And the Devil! That's what you'll inherit!
What then, Sofia? Will you be wiser than me? More
compassionate? Will you show more—

(SOFIA *hesitates, the staff raised.*)

NICOLAS: —Mercy?

(SOFIA *sees the rainbow and gasps.*)

END OF PLAY

www.ingramcontent.com/pod-product-compliance
Lightning Source LLC
Chambersburg PA
CBHW070027110426
42741CB00034B/2668